Leigh Heffer

Leigh

Best wishes to a fellow cat-lover
on her seventh birthday. Hope you
enjoy the beauties in this book.

Love,
Donna + Stephen

Nature Library of Color
CATS AND KITTENS

CRESCENT

When the romantic 1920s novelist Elinor Glyn coined 'It', the alluring quality so attractive to man, which you either had or hadn't, she also said, as a cat owner, "Cats have more natural 'It' than most humans". Whether it is a long-haired cat or a short-haired, sleek or bushy, few people can help but agree with her. Cats have captivated man for thousands of years. They were worshipped as gods and viewed as agents of the devil, and have survived against all odds to secure a permanent place in our homes and hearts.

What is the mystical appeal that cats possess? Most obviously exquisite beauty and grace of movement. Also dignity and independence. But perhaps the greatest attraction lies in their enormous range of emotions that are so similar to ours. Anger, curiosity, contentment, fear, disappointment; all these are feelings that cat owners will agree occur frequently in their cat's life. To coax a cat out of a bad mood is tantamount to helping a friend over a difficult time and to 'own' a cat, if this is possible with such an independent animal, means that another individual is living in the home. Of course they

These appealing bundles of fluff would soften the hardest of hearts: (1) Two white long-haired kittens; (2) white short-haired kitten; (3) tabby short-haired kitten; (4) ginger long-haired kitten with ball; (5) ginger short-haired kitten; (6) tortoiseshell and white long-haired kitten; (7) white short-haired kitten with basket; (8) blue-cream long-haired kitten; (9) ginger and white kitten.

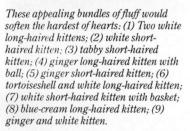

7

8

9

1

2

3

4

5

also have numerous faults. So devious, selfish and arrogant can they sometimes be, it is surprising they have earned any affection at all. But on the occasions when these traits are displayed, apparently genuine repentance makes forgiveness an easy thing, and these flaws are rarely exercised in such a way as to cause genuine harm.

One of the most exasperating facts about cat ownership is how impossible it is to know exactly what is going on inside the feline mind. Anybody who has been scrutinized closely by those piercing eyes, which appear to narrow with some acute perception of your character, will know what it is like to feel that, without reason, you somehow have to justify your actions to your cat. That they are intelligent is undeniable, but to what extent we mould their lives and they ours is difficult to ascertain. It has often been affectionately pointed out that cats allow themselves to be taken into our home and will act the way we want them to for the convenience of regular food and warmth. But this idea does rather paint the picture of an animal, so devious of character, that it could live a permanent lie for some fifteen years without so much as a tiny slip up. More probably, despite their proud and self-contained natures, they are greatly affected by their environment, and the position of equality they demand in the home is born from an inherent sense of leadership. After all, their considerably larger but none the less close relatives do rule the jungle.

Many people see the cat as a small, sometimes cuddly, but in the main relatively ordinary animal that creates noise and diversion when all that is wanted is peace, and it is not always amusing to find a bundle of fur crumpling the newspaper that is just about to be read. But let us stop for a moment to consider the cat's extraordinary history – and try to examine just why we are so pleased when a black cat crosses our path?

Cats and History

Given that cats and dogs bear such apparent animosity towards each other (although this is frequently quite the opposite from the truth), it comes as quite a surprise to discover

Cats and kittens come in many colour combinations: (1) tabby and white shorthair; (2) long-haired blue kitten; (3) long-haired ginger and white kitten; (4) blue-cream short-haired kitten; (5) marmalade longhair; (6) a very popular show-cat, the chinchilla; (7) marmalade shorthair; (8) playful white Persian-cross cat. Overleaf: three adorable kittens – from left to right – long-haired ginger, long-haired cream and short-haired ginger.

that both are descended from a weasel-like creature that lived some fifty million years ago. Over the following ten million years, an animal very similar to modern cats evolved and, apart from various adaptations according to country of habitation, so suited are cats to their environment that they have changed very little since then. Any doubt that they are closely related to the 'big cats' can be quickly dispelled by a visit to the zoo and a quick glance at the majestic lion as it rolls over onto its back for a long and luxurious stretch just like pussy at home. But to be more particular, it is generally considered that domestic cats are directly descended from the smaller wild cats. Although they almost certainly shared ground with man long before the earliest recorded discoveries and were accepted as a form of pest control, first evidence of cats as domesticated animals dates back as far as 1600 BC to the kingdom of Ancient Egypt, so it is likely that the African wildcat was its major ancestor.

The Egyptians showed great respect and affection for their cats. They were venerated as symbols of the gods and to harm them was a crime. It was in cat form that the great sun god Ra overcame the powers of darkness, and there was even a cat goddess called Bast of Pasht whose temple at Bubastis was one of the most magnificent in all Egypt. It has been suggested that 'puss' is derived from 'bast' but it is more likely that 'puss' is an imitation of the cat's hiss. Cats quickly became accustomed to man and it was not long before they entered the household, occupying a position of supreme importance. When a house cat died in Ancient Egypt everyone went into mourning and observed elaborate rites while waiting for another cat to take possession of the empty place.

For hundreds of years, cats enjoyed this revered position all over the world and although evidence of them is missing in Greek mythology, there is no doubt that the Romans considered them invaluable friends. During this time, cats were allowed to roam freely, and wild and domestic strains met and mixed, resulting in the variety of size and colouring of our modern domestic cats. But with the decline of the Roman Empire cats

The garden is a favourite spot for curious kittens, with so much to explore! Red poppies provide a colourful background for this pretty white shorthair (1), while daisies surround the tabby and white shorthair (2). A yellow background highlights the marmalade shorthair (3), with black as the backdrop for the cream

Persian (4). The black and white shorthair finds an empty plant pot full of interesting possibilities (5) and (6), and a disused barrel provides the ideal place from which to investigate the ferns, for the tabby and white shorthair (7).

Engaged in the vital task of grooming is this brown and white tabby (1), while the fierce-looking blue-cream longhair (2) dares anyone to disturb him. In a variety of different settings are (3) tabby and white shorthair; (4) blue-cream short-haired kittens; (5) tabby shorthair; (6) short-haired Siamese kitten; (7) British blue; (8) marmalade short-haired kitten and cream long-haired kitten; (9) an inquisitive marmalade long-haired kitten; (10) a prettily-marked black and white short-haired kitten; and perched on a windowsill, a fluffy cream long-haired kitten (11).

1

2

3

4

suffered. The enigmatic qualities that had previously earned them such respect were suddenly the object of doubt in a frightened and superstitious society. Soon they became associated with the idea of witchcraft and eventually became symbols of evil and misfortune out of all proportion, enduring unspeakable treatment at the hands of men. Hypocritically enough kings, whilst agreeing that cats should be burnt with heretics, made no effort to keep them away from the palaces, and monasteries always kept cats because they freed the place of rodents. Perhaps even more strangely it was at this time that one of history's most famous cats lived. The legendary feline friend of Dick Whittington, Lord Mayor of London.

It was not until the last century that cats finally emerged as delightful and affectionate companions. Few Victorian homes were without their fireside cat, perhaps because it typified comfort and family bliss, and today cats enjoy an increasingly good life, fitting in happily alongside the contemporary symbols of affluence and luxury.

This perky, short-haired tabby watches the world go by (1), while the ginger and white longhair looks too sleepy to watch anything (2). The cross-bred farmhouse tabby (3) is engaged in the grooming and care of her kittens, and looking exceedingly well cared for is the chinchilla kitten on a patchwork quilt (4). A bed of bright red leaves provides a comfortable resting place for the ginger and white shorthair (5), while the farmhouse cat and kitten (6) make do with a bed of straw. The blue tabby Persian kitten (7) nestles into bright green undergrowth.

Kittens

'It is a very convenient habit of kittens (Alice had once made the remark) that, whatever you say to them they *always* purr'.

Lewis Carroll – 'Alice Through the Looking Glass'

Alice's observation was not too far removed from the truth because a kitten has the remarkable knack of gaining full enjoyment out of every possible situation. At its worst a kitten is a delightful ball of fluff that demands a lot of attention, so consider how endearing it is at its best. Without fail it captivates cat-lovers and non cat-lovers alike. But when it is born, unable to see its surroundings and struggling to find its mother's milk, it is by no means a pretty thing. It will be at least ten to fourteen days before liquid-blue eyes will be staring trustingly up at you and the cuddly kitten will attempt to take its first wander. At this stage a kitten is still heavily dependent on its mother who will teach it how to wash, play and hunt. Naturally inquisitive, its exaggerated expressions and clumsy antics are irresistible. To see a kitten encountering a shoe for the first time or to catch sight of its little face in the garden, peeping round the daffodils that tower menacingly overhead is pure delight. So it is at this stage that the biggest word of warning must be given to prospective cat owners. As Ogden Nash pointed out – 'The trouble with a kitten is THAT. Eventually it becomes a CAT'. This means, if the cat remains healthy all its life, that more than fourteen years of taking care of an animal which loses its 'kitten appeal' fairly quickly faces the owner. If the prospect of this is daunting then however perfect a gift a kitten would make for your child, harden your heart and resist the temptation to buy on impulse – there are already too many unwanted cats who find themselves on the street at a very early age. If you do buy a kitten it is advisable to have it doctored unless breeding is specifically in mind. A male cat is by nature a fighter and will spend a large proportion of its time marking out its territory (which includes the house) by spraying on the chosen areas. At

Tabbies are recognised by, amongst other characteristics, the distinct "M" mark on the forehead. Pedigrees are classically marked with rings on the legs and tail, and swirls of pattern on the flanks, and they display not a single white hair. The majority of house pets are cross-breeds or mongrels, recognised by their white chests, or legs or both, although, as these pictures show, they are no less appealing.

3

4

2

5

6

7

These blue-eyed cream and ginger long-haired kittens (1) make a delightful picture against the blue and tan background. The height of the cyclamen shows how tiny this silver tabby kitten is (2). Gardens provide an attractive setting for a tabby mother and her kittens (3), white and tabby shorthair kittens (4), and this pensive silver tabby shorthair (5). The brightly-coloured background highlights this tabby longhair (6), whose fluffy coat contrasts strongly with the sleek, shiny fur of the Birman and Burmese kittens, pictured here in a tangle of ears, paws and eyes (7).

night it will roam the streets trying to attract females or 'queens' by caterwauling, which to a human would seem enough to turn away any potential sweetheart! But not so the undoctored female cat. She will do anything in her power to get outside when on heat and attempts to keep her in the house often prove fruitless, particularly as it is not always easy to identify when these times occur. If you have your kitten doctored, and the best time is considered to be between four and six months, none of these problems will cause concern when the kitten matures. Should you find an unwanted litter on your hands, take the kittens to the vet to be put down; drowning is painful and cruel, even to a kitten only a few hours old.

So, having taken all this into account, you go ahead and buy a kitten. Even at this age, which should not be less than about ten weeks, it will be developing the ability to skilfully manipulate circumstances to its own advantage, much like an unscrupulous dealer in business. A kitten will turn its nose up at food it doesn't like and if the food is never offered again, will grow into an extremely fussy eater who has realised at an early age that everything it wants, it gets. Offer the food again a few days later and it may well be quickly eaten up, no trace of the earlier dislike to be seen. Of course there are some popular myths, when it comes to food, that should be discounted. Not all cats like fish, or milk, and certainly neither is imperative to their diet. Ultimately, if a cat really doesn't like something and it is not just a kittenish fad, it will never eat it, so there is little point in persisting.

A kitten may be fussy in its food but when it comes to attention, all, without exception, seek it. The more attention you lavish on a kitten, the more devoted it will become to you, both then and in adulthood. And how heartwarming it is to have this little creature curled up contentedly in your lap or bounding playfully towards you when you enter the room.

Enjoy the pleasure of your kitten and it will reward you by being an equally enjoyable companion for many years to come.

Different Breeds

The problem of what breed of kitten to buy does not usually worry most people. Character is the most sought-after quality and there is no evidence to suggest that a pure-bred is in any way superior to a cross-bred. If, however, a pedigree cat is required there is a bewildering choice and the ultimate decision is a matter of purely personal taste. If expert advice is needed then it is best to consult a breeder.

Abyssinian, Manx, Chinchilla, Burmese, Persian and Siamese are just a few of the many breeds available. Cats do not vary tremendously in size or domestic requirements, so the first choice that must be made is – should it be long-haired or short-haired? The short-haired group can be divided into those known as British (or Domestic in America), Foreign or Oriental and the Manx. By far the most popular are the graceful Siamese, brought to Britain from Siam some ninety years ago. Their sleek cream coats are most usually tipped with seal-brown, but

Inquisitive, playful or serene – some of the many facets of a cat's personality are captured here. (1) Persian cross-breed; (2) watchful Siamese; (3) tabby kitten; (4) white Persian; (5) cautious marmalade kitten; (6) cross-bred tabby kitten, making his presence felt! Freed from his basket is the white shorthair (7), while finding plenty to occupy themselves are the seal-point Siamese (8), the blue shorthair (9) and the blue-cream longhair (10).

6

7

8

9

10

1

2

3

4

5

the points can also be tabby, blue, chocolate, tortoiseshell or red. Most Siamese are excellent hunters, extremely independent and notorious for stealing food. Although they love company they do not always earn favour as they have a noticeably low regard for household furniture, unlike the Burmese who are similar in temperament but very affectionate, less noisy and considerably more gentle. Another popular short-haired breed is the Abyssinian, probably nearest to the cats of Ancient Egypt. Either rabbit-coloured or red, they are extremely intelligent and capable of great affection, although it may be specifically directed only at the owner. Then there are the Manx cats, with variously-coloured coats and quite unique in that they are tail-less. The origins of these cats are a complete mystery. Some say that many years ago their tails were cut off to decorate the shields of Irish warriors and to prevent this happening the mother cats bit off their babies' tails at birth. Another story says these cats are descended from the tail-less Spanish cats, three of which hid in the hold of one of the retreating Armada ships and swam ashore near Port Erin in the Isle of Man. But perhaps the most amusing anecdote comes from the Bible. It seems that the Manx was the last of

(1) Sleepy-eyed Birman and Burmese kittens snuggle into each other, while the orange-eyed white Persian kitten peeps around the corner (2). Basking in the sun is this white shorthair (3), a complete contrast to the two alert tabby longhairs (4). The adorable fluffy kittens are: (5) marmalade shorthair; (6) long-haired tabby and cream kittens; (8) black and white shorthair; with long-haired silver tabby kittens overleaf. Brown velvet shows off the lustrous coat of this cream longhair to perfection (7).

causing a furball. This is why cats sometimes eat grass. It acts as a natural emetic and helps to bring up the furball. If grooming is introduced as a daily routine soon after a kitten has arrived in the home it will be accepted quickly and often looked forward to with pleasure. A soft bristle brush and two combs, one with fine teeth to catch any fleas that may be harboured in the coat and the other with wider teeth for general combing, is all that is needed. Before brushing starts, the coat must be freed from any tangles and this is best done by hand. Then comb and brush firmly all over, finishing with vigorous hand stroking. Any bad tangles will have to be cut away very carefully, using round ended scissors. Dirt which has collected in the ears or in the corner of the eyes should be very

1

2

gently wiped away with cotton wool. Following these simple instructions will ensure that a cat remains at its best. However there are various infections that need expert treatment. All cats must be vaccinated against feline infectious enteritis, initially, and preferably, between two and

Healthy, active and alert cats make interesting pets, like the white shorthair (2) and (5); the two cream longhairs (1); beautifully-marked brown tabbies (4) and (7); the bushy-tailed marmalade (6); and the pensive blue-cream (8). Kittens scrabble for their mother's milk (3).

3

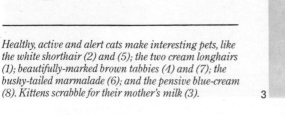

5

6

7

8

1

2

3

4

5

three months of age, with a booster injection each year. More often than not the effects of this highly-contagious disease are fatal and the vet must be consulted at the slightest suspicion.

Eyes and ears are also frequent targets for infection, often as a result of injuries sustained during a fight or a fall. Again these are best dealt with by a vet, and it is a good idea to find a vet near to your home so that he can build up a medical history of your cat from the beginning which will be of great help on subsequent visits. Always telephone first because simple advice on how to treat the ailment may be all that is necessary, or, more importantly, the infection may be contagious and the vet will not want you entering the surgery by the waiting room where there are other animals. Worms are common and relatively simple to treat. There are several products on the market that, providing they are made by a reputable company, will clear up the infection quickly, but make sure the medicine is specifically designed for cats as even a simple aspirin, the cure for a multitude of human aches and pains, can prove fatal.

If there is any doubt about your cat's health do not fail to consult a vet – the only person with the correct training and facilities to deal with it.

Personality

It is impossible to generalise about the personalities of cats. A quick glance through the many poems and stories that have been written about them will show that there are cool cats, affectionate cats, clever cats and unbelievably stupid ones, lively cats and lazy ones. No sooner is it written that all cats like sitting on laps than someone will come up with a little anecdote about their cat who will not even stay in the house for more than half an hour, let alone nestle down comfortably in a lap. Despite this, certain characteristics do seem to be fairly universal throughout the cat kingdom. Cats are remarkably independent creatures. It may not always show because, unlike humans, they are not going to fight for independence when there is no need to. But they can, and will, fend for themselves. One cat, born and brought up in the heart of the country

6

Siamese cats are most popular these days, and are identified by "points"–these (1) are lilac-points. The tiny marmalade kitten (2) and (3) becomes an intrepid explorer in an overgrown garden. Deep red backgrounds provide a rich contrast to the beautiful coats of the long-haired blue and cream kittens (4); the blue Persian kittens (5); and an exquisite chinchilla (6).

1

3

4

2

5

and much loved by her owners, was nowhere to be found, when, as the final stages of a move to a big city arrived, they searched everywhere for her. Eventually there was nothing to be done but to go without her and ask the neighbours to keep a watchful eye on her comings and goings and place food out every day. Six months later, on a special trip just to find the wayward pussy, the family went to the neighbours first, who said there had been virtually no sign of her. But on arriving at the doorstep of their old house, out shot the cat, slightly bedraggled but exceptionally fit and obviously delighted to see them. Today, ten years later, she sits, watching the traffic pass by from her post by the window of the house in the city, and occasionally investigates the small garden at the back of the house. No doubt she's decided it's much too much bother fending for herself!

Another feline characteristic is changeable moods. In a recent radio interview, an astrologer revealed that he had come to the conclusion that cats, like humans, are affected by the star sign under which they are born.

If this is the case then most cats, whether Scorpio, Taurus or whatever, seem to have more than a hint of Gemini in them! Impulsive in their decision making; as quick to like one thing as they are to dislike the very same thing a day later; capable of intense devotion, (although many people have affectionately commented that this devotion appears strongest at feeding time) and totally confident that, by fair means or foul, they will get what they want. Perhaps the notion of cat-astrology is a little far-fetched but certainly all cats have very distinct personalities.

Curiosity

Curiosity, so the old proverb goes, killed the cat. But considering that another proverb blesses the cat with having nine lives, this provides ample

Blue backgrounds contrast with the pale fur of a long-haired cream kitten (1) an orange-eyed Persian kitten (6) and the short-haired tabby and white cat (4). Two ginger and white kittens scamper in the garden (2), while the windowsill provides a perfect site from which to watch the world go by for the blue shorthair (3) and the tabby longhair and tortoiseshell shorthair (7). (5) Black and white kitten with fuschia.

opportunity for them to nose around. And nose around they certainly will. Even if they live in a tiny flat there will always be something worth exploring. They will want to get to the top of the highest cupboard, inside the smallest drawer, see if they can balance on the thinnest window ledge and above all, find it totally imperative to identify anything that moves and deal with it accordingly. This insatiable desire to know everything that is going on, in much the same way as a village gossip, can not only provide the opportunity for catching your cat at its most amusing, perhaps when circling an old shoe and patting it to see whether it moves, but can also lead to some very sticky situations, and it is debatable whether cats are quite so adventurous when the owners are not around to give a helping hand. However, cats do have an exceptional sense of self-preservation and it is highly unlikely that objects or new territory will be investigated unless there is an escape route, however slim the chances of one may appear to the human observer. A particularly bulky tabby that normally found it just a little bit too much effort to jump onto the window sill, let alone anything higher, was once found, to the horror of its owner, poised precariously between the chimney stacks on a very high roof. The fire-brigade was called but no sooner did they arrive than the cat, obviously tired of the view, confidently found its way down to the ground and walked off, head held high, towards the house.

If, for any reason, you don't want your cat to explore a certain cupboard, any attempt to stop it will almost invariably enhance its curiosity. Similarly there is little point in trying to show your cat what is inside the carrier bag that its eyes are so mischievously fixed upon. It will want to find out for itself and will probably sit washing, feigning total lack of interest until you leave the thing alone. In kittenhood, much as with a young child, it is as well to keep a watchful eye on these inquisitive antics. A kitten's powers of patience amount to very little and it will go rushing headlong into, onto or under anything, only to be saved from trouble by a mournful mew.

Goldfish fascinate a long-haired tabby (1), while the white shorthair kitten is fascinated by beautiful cerise flowers (2). Peeping through lacy curtains is a blue-cream longhair (3). Kittens are always appealing, like the two cream longhairs (4) and the brown tabby shorthair (5); two tabby and white kittens snuggle into mother (6). At play or on the prowl—these tabby and white cats (7) and (8) are attractively marked.

4

5

6

7

8

1

As with everything a cat does, it is not always easy to distinguish between the innocently curious or deviously clever methods of attracting attention. To a large extent this will depend on the mood you are in and whether or not you have the time and the inclination to play. Often, if you have all the time in the world, everything else in the house will be of interest to your cat except you. Equally well, if you are hurriedly scribbling out a note for the milkman before going out, the moving end of the pencil will be the focus of pussy's attention (and paws). Without doubt the trailing plant that you are attempting to repot suddenly needs thorough investigation and as for the hem you are trying to stitch up for this evening's party – it may as well be abandoned!

(1) A beautiful wide-eyed long-haired ginger kitten gazes into the distance, while the bi-coloured shorthair finds something outside his window to fascinate him (2). (3) and (6) Tabby and white is a most attractive combination, particularly in this young shorthair. Kittens and their mothers always make a lovely picture, whether in luxurious surroundings or a humble barn (4) and (5).

At Work...

These days it would be forgivable to comment that the word 'work' occupies no place in the feline vocabulary – unless of course work consists of searching out new territory for a more comfortable sleep and keeping your coat scrupulously clean. But a quick flick through the chapters of history will reveal that this was not always the case. As Ted Hughes suggests in 'How the Cat Came to Live with Man' it was because of its indispensable skills as a worker that it first found a place in human society.

'Man was so surprised to see Cat that at first he just stood…Cat spoke first. "I've come for a job", he said…"You look as if you'd make a fine rat-catcher", said Man…' no doubt having caught sight of 'Cat's' sharp teeth and long claws. Even in Ancient Egypt it is plausible that the god Ra, represented by a cat killing the serpent Apep (darkness), was not purely symbolic but indicative of the fact that cats became skilled at killing the snakes which threatened the granaries. Certainly by the end of the fourth century AD in Europe cats were fully established as useful pest killers. Unfortunately, during the Middle Ages when cats became linked with witchcraft they were considered more of a risk to fertility than a help, with the disastrous result that the church denounced the cat and all who associated with it. The effect of this was a substantial increase in the rat population and when the plague arrived, vermin carried it freely far and wide. The cat quickly re-emerged as a useful animal and from then on earned increasing appreciation and affection from its human companions.

Today many urban cats are notorious loungers, occasionally catching birds or flies if the mood takes them. But in country areas thousands of cats do a good day's work and are rewarded for it with regular food and shelter – on farms,

(1) Seal-point Siamese; (2) red leaves of autumn highlight the coat of this ginger and white shorthair; (3) a basketful of fluff! (4) and (7) marmalade kitten peering through the undergrowth; (5) tabby and white shorthair; (6) long-haired cream kitten; (8) magnificent example of red Persian; (9) aristocratic lilac-point Siamese; (10) blue Persian kitten.

1

2

3

4

in factories, restaurants and churches and of course as the familiar 'pub cat' whose job usually entails entertaining customers rather than catching mice. A little country pub, due to its rustic location, was frequently troubled by mice in the cellars and, as a last resort, the owners invested in a cat whom they called Jasper. They laid down the laws on a very definite basis and Jasper soon learned that the more mice he caught the more he would be in favour with the owners and be allowed inside the house to sit by the fire. But if mice were spotted and Jasper was seen elsewhere sleeping or washing himself, he was left out at night to fend for himself. On this basis, the months went by and very soon there was not a mouse to be found. Delighted with this, the

Beautiful garden flowers provide a perfect setting for these two bundles of fur. Above Tabby and white shorthair; *left* white longhair.

owners allowed Jasper into their pub to mix with the customers. As time progressed the owners became aware that Jasper seemed to spend all his time indoors and still there was no sign of any mice. After thorough investigation the owners discovered that Jasper had used the art of delegation and that a stray from the village was being 'employed' by him to keep the mice away in return for a few scraps of food that Jasper brought out late at night after everybody had gone to bed!

It is not only on land that cats prove useful. Despite the fact that they are not supposed to like water, Dick Whittington's legendary cat was reputed to have cleared not only a ship of rats, but a whole island, and Japanese sailors believed cats could tell if storms were brewing and could ward them off, so usually carried one aboard.

...and at Play

Whether play means to a cat what it means to its human owners is questionable. As with a baby, almost any activity which is not concerned with feeding, sleeping or washing can be construed as play and it is only as the cat matures that playing can be more easily discriminated from other activities. Running, jumping, catching, hiding; during all these a cat displays charming characteristics which are a delight to watch and would be considered as play in our world. But one fact which becomes obvious after watching kittens at play is that it is instinctive, and a vital way of learning skills which are required in adult life. The well-known stalking procedure which can be quite terrifying in a fully grown cat is, at the early stage, enchanting as the kitten crouches low to the ground, swaying to and fro in mock menace. This is encouraged by the mother bringing in small catches from outside for the kitten to play around with and she will often allow it to practice this predatory instinct on her twitching tail. A ball of wool can provide endless hours of enjoyment but it must be remembered that a kitten will invariably chew things and may swallow certain objects that are highly dangerous. A cat may not play as much as it gets older but, particularly if it is an indoor cat, will continue to indulge in games much as we would pick up a book to fill some time or play a game of tennis to keep fit. But just how playful a cat will be, who they will play with and what sort of games they wish to play, is largely dependent on its breed, upbringing and individual personality. One cat may prefer to play on its own and is wicked enough to gain most pleasure from playing with something you are using. Another will be far more easily pleased, spending hours trying to scoop a cotton reel out from under the sofa. If a cat is provided with its own toys, perhaps a toy mouse stuffed with catnip (a herb which

Cats and kittens at play. (1) Tabby and white kitten crouches in the grass, while the marmalade kitten (2) climbs over a handy log. Building blocks provide amusement for these ginger and cream kittens (3). (4) Blue Persian. (5) and (6) Tabby and white, marmalade and blue-cream kittens join forces to make sure that every inch of the garden is explored. Black and white kitten (7) and blue-cream kitten (9) frolic happily in the garden. Staring impassively is this magnificent cream longhair (8).

1

2

3

4

5

6

Balanced on the arm of a chair is a marmalade longhair kitten, while his companion, a cream longhair, rests on the cushion (1). The garden becomes a refuge for a white short-haired kitten (2), but a basket provides comfort for the lilac

Burmese kitten (3). Blue sets off the blue eyes of this beautiful white longhair (4), while shadow stripes the attractively marked tabby (5). The black and white kitten (6) has obviously decided that he needs some attention!

sends some cats into ecstasy) it will stalk it, bite it in the neck and triumphantly throw it up into the air again and again. A plastic ball may be more suitable for a kitten as it is difficult to chew up. After a short time, a cat can become very adept at football, manoeuvring the ball skilfully around chair legs and along window ledges, patting it expertly from paw to paw. If there is another cat in the house (or any other animal that has been brought up with the cat from an early age) they will almost certainly enjoy playing together and a kitten always seems happiest when romping around with its litter mates than when left to its own devices.

Cats in Photography

How many times have you sat at home and watched your kitten having a wrestling match with a cotton reel on the floor, or caught sight of your large tabby stalking a pigeon in the garden and wished that you could capture that precious moment for ever? All those naturally appealing postures and charming expressions would be strong competition for even the best models when it comes to attractive pictures, and many an actor would benefit from possessing the dramatic skills of a cat. It is little wonder therefore, that cats have found themselves a secure job in the professional photographer's studio. Pictures of fluffy kittens staring innocently out from the lids of chocolate boxes persuade the onlooker that the contents of the box are as sweet and attractive as the kittens are. Greetings cards, calendars and magazine covers too are frequently adorned with delightful cats, whilst the real actors advertise tins of their very own food on the television screen.

Obviously, the more natural a photograph of a cat looks, the more it will appeal to us. But as every professional animal photographer knows, these apparently spontaneous pictures often take hours of filming and require an unlimited amount of patience to capture just the right moment before the subject gets bored and wanders off, or its expression changes. Everybody knows that it is relatively simple to obtain an acceptable snapshot of the family pet,

1

2

3

and you may even be lucky enough to catch one of those magical moments when the cat endears itself to you so strongly. But to consistently produce good quality colour photographs with the animals carefully arranged in an attractive position for commercial purposes is not an easy job. A still-life arrangement may take hours to set up, but once it is in the correct position, in that position it will stay and the photographer can take as much time as is necessary to produce

a good picture of it. Where cats and kittens are concerned exactly the opposite is true. Their insatiable curiosity, mischievous natures and wilful independence will make it extremely difficult for the photographer to set a cat down in any one position and hope that it will stay that way until the photograph has been taken. Certain standard procedures before the photography begins can, however, help this particular problem. The subject itself, for instance, will rarely be used for preliminary focusing. A toy animal of comparable size is often placed in the right position while the lighting and other technical details are being arranged and then it will be removed and replaced, hopefully by the real thing. If there is no preconceived idea of the exact picture required, the

Orange feathers contrast with the pale coat of this tiny lilac Burmese kitten (1). A blue Burmese mother prepares to feed her kittens (2). Honeysuckle frames this picture of two marmalade kittens (3), while the marmalade kitten (4) and (5)

plays in the manner of all young kittens. Perched on a dark-green velvet chair, the black and white long-haired kitten (6) and (8) gazes serenely around him, while the young tabby kitten (7) is anything but serene!

photographer could take a series of shots featuring the cat doing precisely what it would like to do and then choose the most appealing picture afterwards. More often than not however, a specific posture in one specific place is required.

It becomes apparent then, that taking a professional photograph of a cat or kitten involves not only the skills of the photographer but an element of luck. If a cat does not want to play the 'game' it simply will not do so. Any attempts to scold or punish it in any way to make it co-operate will usually make matters worse and even if the cat does finally do what is asked of it, a frightened or angry expression does not make a particularly delightful picture.

Most successful animal photographers have a good understanding of the animals that they are dealing with. Some will play

Kittens everywhere! (1) Two cream longhairs; (2) cream longhairs and blue longhairs; (3) white Persian; (4) tabby shorthairs; (5) cream longhair and blue longhairs; (6) white longhair; (7) seal-point Siamese; (8) black longhair; (9) tabby and white shorthair.

with a kitten before a photography session to establish a good relationship and ultimately, the animal's trust and confidence. There is little point in attempting to sit a cat down in a certain position straight away and hope to take a perfect picture the first time. If a relationship is established first, the photographer will have a better chance of anticipating the cat's reactions to what is going to be asked of it. But even this period of playing requires experience. It would be all too easy to wear a kitten out before taking any shots at all, and if the picture

1

2

3

4

5

6

required is of an alert, lively kitten, achieving the best result may take a lot longer than originally expected!

Having made apparent the difficulties that can be experienced photographing just one cat or kitten, it is simple to imagine the complications of attempting to photograph two, three or more kittens. If a bundle of playful, mischievous fur is desired then perhaps all will turn out well. To have them all sitting respectfully, staring appealingly into the camera will be a more tricky job, and a very entertaining one to watch!

The Senses

Cats, like many animals, have extremely highly-developed senses. Their whiskers and paws are essential as instruments of touch. Their ears prick up at the slightest noise. Their sight is keen both night and day and their sense of smell is an important factor in identifying objects and asessing food.

SIGHT. Being a nocturnal creature it might be thought that a cat relies more heavily on its other senses for moving around but this is not the case. A cat's eyes are specifically designed to extract full potential from any light available. The pupil opens or closes to allow the correct amount of light through to the retina in order to form a clear picture. In a normal eye, light that passes through the retina and does not stimulate the receptor cells first time round is lost. In a cat's eyes a layer of silvery crystals, called the tapetum, behind the retina, acts as a reflector, providing another opportunity for the cells to be stimulated by the rays; hence a cat can 'see in the dark'. If you shine a light directly into a cat's eyes, they will emit a characteristic glow, and this is the tapetum reflecting the rays of light back. During the day the pupils contract to protect the eyes by excluding the full rays of the sun. Research shows that cats are not able to distinguish colours well, but during the day a cat can often see colours more clearly than at night.

SMELL. By using the sensitive receptor cells in its nasal membrane and combining the information

7

8

(1) Ginger and cream longhair; (2) ginger longhair with ball; (3) "pussies in a well"; (4) tiny blue-cream among the daisies; (5) pensive tortoiseshell; (6) female cross-breed; (7) elegant cream longhair; (8) slightly off-balance tabby!

received with a keenly developed sense of taste, a cat will know immediately what food it likes. Certain herbs and perfumes appeal strongly to a cat and it will also use its sense of smell when investigating objects. But most importantly a cat can tell, by smelling the air, whether another cat, even if it is a long way off, is male or female, and a tom will avoid the territory of another tomcat by picking up the scent of the urine that has marked the ground.

HEARING. The higher the frequency of a noise, the more actively a cat will respond, which perhaps explains why it reacts more readily to a woman's voice. In the wild cats use their sense of hearing for locating prey and sensing danger. In the home a cat quickly learns the sounds that directly concern it, such as its food bowl being placed on the floor. It will also learn the sound of its own name (although this it will frequently ignore) and associates the tone of your voice with whether you are pleased or displeased. It was recently discovered that all-white cats with blue eyes are usually deaf, although if they have even two coloured hairs, or if one of the eyes is a different colour, then hearing is normal. The reason for this is not known for certain but it does not seem to affect their hunting, or their relationships with other cats.

TOUCH. The eye-brows, hairs lining the ear and on the cheek, whiskers and paws are known to be extremely sensitive in cats. The real function of the whiskers is a slight mystery, but as soon as the cat starts to move they are brought forward well in front of its face and will twitch, feeling for obstacles. If they are cut off, a cat is temporarily incapacitated.

The Hunter

She sights a Bird – she chuckles –
She flattens – then she crawls –
She runs without the look of feet –
Her eyes increase to Balls –
Often, as the cat did in that poem, urban cats unused to hunting lose their prey, but cats are carnivores and in the wild, kill for food. It is hardly surprising then that such an innately strong instinct has never died even in the cat that does not

(1) White shorthair kitten among the buttercups – does he like butter? (2) In a more dramatic setting is this exquisite white Persian; (3) tongue protruding in absolute concentration, the long-haired tabby stares out of the window; (4) another taking the buttercup test is this tabby and white kitten; (5) black and white kitten; (6) tabby-point Siamese; (7) a bagful of mischief – three cream long-haired kittens.

need to fend for itself. A superbly-equipped hunter – its stealthiness, sharp teeth and claws are specially designed for catching small prey, and even a cat who is deprived of outdoor hunting will use the same patterns of behaviour when playing with a toy or exploring new territory.

To watch a cat hunting is a fascinating experience. In urban areas the prey is most likely to be a mouse or a small insect but in country districts a cat will hunt rabbits, hares, frogs and fish. Even a strange noise will put it on the alert because when it senses danger the same hunting pattern emerges in order to discover the source of the threat. At other times, particularly in the home, there appears to be no good reason for a cat's actions and its ears may prick up at the slightest sound, apparently being able to read into it far more than we can. At times like this, it would be interesting to know what the cat is thinking. It may be washing when suddenly it will freeze, a paw perhaps suspended in mid-air, ears pricked, eyes scanning the room. Sometimes it will dash for safety or lose interest, but at other times the predatory instinct will emerge. Muscles taught, senses alert, it moves, body crouched low to the ground, to a position where it can observe its prey but is itself concealed. Almost bewitched, it watches the prey's every movement, deep in a world of its own far removed from playing with balls of wool or stretching luxuriously in front of the fire. At this point we are helpless bystanders, graciously allowed to watch but useless if we try to actively participate. As the cat pads noiselessly from one concealed spot to another its prey is totally unaware of its presence. If the cat encounters any open ground it will soundlessly dash across to the next shaded or covered area and crouch low again, ears flattened against the head and whiskers and tail twitching in anticipation. Reaching a point close enough to make the 'kill', it will abruptly halt, freeze and wait for just the right moment. The final stage consists of a short run, a lightning-quick pounce and a bite on the back of the neck which, if successful, kills instantaneously. The killing action is learnt in kittenhood. The fact that

1

2

3

4

5

mothers carry the kittens by the neck indicates that this is the best way to control an animal if it fights back, and a trapped animal almost certainly will. It is now that we see the cat at its most tyrannical and it is often hard to believe that you are watching the same cat that only an hour ago was rubbing affectionately against your legs. It ruthlessly torments the creature, throwing it high in the air or keeping a paw on its tail almost daring it to get away. Before you are tempted to step in, and prise your cat away from its hapless prey, it must be remembered that, however human your cat's emotions may appear to be, this is one area in which we share no understanding. What it is doing is only cruel by human standards and is a deeply-rooted part of its nature and an accepted act in the animal kingdom. Christopher Smart was more benevolent about this feline trait when it came to his cat Jeoffrey, attributing to it fair play and good sportsmanship. 'For when he takes his prey he plays with it to give it a chance…' This may be so with Jeoffrey but hunting is a game which most cats are not too happy to lose!

Perched on a bale of straw is this delightful Persian cross (1); and the beautifully-marked black and white kitten gazes into middle distance, against a deep blue background (2) and (3). A fur-covered black chair provides a striking background to the lilac and brown Burmese kittens (4). Paws draped over purple velvet, this magnificent silver tabby kitten gazes wide-eyed away from the camera (5). As splendidly-marked as the plants around him is the bi-colour kitten (6), while the garden again is a perfect play area for the white shorthair (7) and (9) and the tabby and white (8). Overleaf ginger and cream kittens find amusement in the kitchen.

1

2

3

4

As a final gesture, if your cat is particularly devoted to you, it may include you in the excitement by placing the dead mouse or some other creature at your feet. This action combines affection and the desire to be praised. However squeamish you are, do try to humour your cat. Better a dead mouse on the carpet which can be disposed of in seconds than a huffy cat that may shun you for days!

The Good Companion

How many times have you been asked 'Are you a cat-person or a dog-person?' Traditionally it seems that liking one constitutes utter loathing, or at best toleration, of the other. Rough-and-ready outdoor people are supposed to like dogs and comfort-seekers are thought to feel an instant affinity with the cat. Of course this is patently untrue and there are many examples of people who have been devoted to both animals to prove it. Winston Churchill for instance, who wept when his poodle Rufus died, was notorious for having his marmalade cat present at wartime cabinet meetings. Thousands of households contain a dog and a cat who live in perfect harmony with each other and their owners. However, if you are actively seeking a companion when you decide to buy an animal then vast differences in temperament certainly do exist between a cat and a dog. Why people seek companionship from animals can perhaps be attributed in part to a sense of social inferiority, a fear of rejection in relationships with fellow men. Animals do not present this threat of rejection unless they are rejected themselves. Once a person is inside his own home he is assured that his pet will accept him for what he is without question. A dog in its natural environment, however, is used to being a member of a pack and obeying the laws laid down by the leader. In the home it is this sort of relationship with its master that will bring out the best in it. A cat, on the other hand, is a solitary creature, confident in itself and, under natural conditions, relatively ungregarious. A cat will respect your authority if it appears to have good reason and respond best to being treated as an equal, not as an object to fulfil your

Two of the most beautiful varieties of cat are the chinchilla (1) and the silver tabby (2). Siamese and white kittens pose enchantingly (3). Mother grooms her kittens (4) and a brown Burmese kitten chews his basket (5). Long-haired ginger kittens (6) groom each other.

5

6

desires. It can fend for itself and is not a faithful friend come-what-may who will weaken under the exertion of power.

A dog can very easily be trained to perform all kinds of tricks to order. A cat, although equally, if not more intelligent, very soon indicates that the learning of tricks is beneath its dignity. It is quite capable of performing these tricks and will do so, for your pleasure if the mood takes it, but any attempt to order a cat to do anything will meet with a frosty reception.

To secure a cat as a friend, therefore, and not just as a resident guest, is not easy. It does not intend to be understood, although it is secretly rather pleased if you do see through its evasive image to the affectionate nature underneath. It has complex emotions and is frequently guilty of the most blatant cupboard love. As its provider you have not necessarily earned its genuine affection – a cat is quite capable of biting the hand that feeds it and it will unhesitatingly turn its back on a home or a person who does not suit it, disappearing for several days at a time, or altogether. How good a companion it is depends largely on you as the owner. Obviously temperament does differ according to breed but if you lavish attention on any cat it will usually return it ten-fold. If you establish a pattern from kittenhood of playing for ten minutes when you come home it will look forward to your return every day and perhaps wait at the door to greet you with a nuzzle and a purr. But cats are very sensitive and you cannot afford to play around with their emotions. If love is given one day and withdrawn the next, consistently and over a period of time, you will eventually lose its trust and forfeit its affection.

There are many remarkable stories which illustrate just how good a companion a cat can be. Perhaps the most touching is of the cat who 'adopted' an old lady many years ago. They became inseparable as time passed and wherever the old lady went, so did the cat. As the old lady became increasingly housebound, concerned neighbours would call on her to make sure all was well but they soon realised that, as the cat was invariably by her side if they ever saw it in the garden it usually meant

All kittens use play to teach themselves about life–they stalk imaginary prey, play hide and seek, learn to relate to one another, and how to define territory. These lessons form the basis for their future lives.

something was wrong. One morning the cat was sitting outside so the neighbours went round to see if anything was wrong. They found the old lady at the bottom of the stairs, unable to get up because of a fall. They took her to hospital where it was discovered that she had broken a hip and would have to be hospitalised for quite some time. The neighbours returned home with the promise that they would look after the cat, but when they returned it was nowhere to be seen. It had found its way to the hospital and was sitting mournfully outside the ward in which the old lady had been placed. Over the next few days the cat remained in the vicinity, and although not allowed in, patiently waited for its mistress to be discharged. When she left and returned home it was there waiting for her on her arrival.

This sort of devotion is quite rare, but it serves to show that cats are capable of great affection. They often provide warmth and love at times when it is most needed, without recriminations or questions. Enjoy their company, keep them happy and well-looked after and it will be a pleasure to have one in the home.

Cream or white, black or grey, tabby or tortoiseshell, a moggy or a prize pedigree, every cat owner or cat lover has his favourite. Each pet is an individual with endearing habits and winning ways. Cuddly kittens grow into sleek, independent cats – not too independent, though; they soon learn how to manage the best of both worlds! Whatever their personality, they capture the hearts of all who know them.

First English edition published in 1981 by Colour Library International Ltd.
This edition is published by Crescent Books, Distributed by Crown Publishers Inc.
Illustrations and text © : Colour Library International Ltd. 163 East 64th Street, New York 10021.
Colour separations by FERCROM, Barcelona, Spain.
Display and text filmsetting by Focus Photoset, London, England.
Printed by Cayfosa and bound by Eurobinder - Barcelona (Spain)
All rights reserved.
Library of Congress Catalog Card Number: 81-67587
CRESCENT 1981

Dep. Leg. B. 1.265/82